ANGIE DEBO

DAUGHTER OF THE PRAIRIE:
WITH EXCERPTS FROM HER CHILDHOOD DIARY

PATRICIA LOUGHLIN

I AM OKLAHOMA
CHILDREN'S SERIES

SERIES EDITOR: GINI MOORE CAMPBELL

OKLAHOMA HALL *of* FAME
PUBLISHING

OKLAHOMA HALL *of* FAME

2017 OFFICERS AND DIRECTORS

The Oklahoma Hall of Fame would like to thank Darleen Bailey Beard, Pati Hailey, Gwendolyn Hooks, Jane McKellips, and Cheryl Schuermann—the founding five authors of the I Am Oklahoma Children's Series—for their creation of and investment in this series to celebrate Oklahoma's best and brightest with our state's youngest citizens.

ANGIE DEBO
DAUGHTER OF THE PRAIRIE
WITH EXCERPTS FROM HER CHILDHOOD DIARY

Foreword by Robert Henry with Penny Williams 7

Introduction 8

Chapter 1   Daughter of the Prairie 11

Chapter 2   Going to School 18

Chapter 3   Coming to Oklahoma 21

Chapter 4   Making Oklahoma Home 30

Conclusion   Historical Significance of Angie Debo 34

Glossary 38

Places to Visit 38

Timeline 39

Bibliography 40

Index 40

Artist Charles Banks Wilson and historian Angie Debo with her portrait in her home in Marshall, 1985. During the 1980s state representatives Robert Henry and Penny Williams advocated to have Angie Debo's portrait commissioned by the state of Oklahoma for the State Art Collection and is on display in the Oklahoma State Capitol Rotunda. *Courtesy Angie Debo Collection, Archives, OSU Library, Oklahoma State University, Stillwater.*

Foreword
By Robert Henry with Penny Williams

There are few people in our history who have done more to preserve the dignity, **culture**, history, and contributions of our first Americans than Angie Debo. She would indeed be honored to know of this book. A student all her life, even as she taught others, she would be humbled to think that her life and her amazing drive might be an inspiration to other young women and men. Hers was the first portrait of a woman hung in our historic Oklahoma State Capitol.

This remarkable woman, beginning with a childhood diary, had used her written words to lead the charge to protect the rights of Indians, women, minorities, and those unfairly treated by our legal system. Her remarkable prose led to the publication of a baker's dozen of books, scores of articles, and later documentaries.

This book tells the story of a little girl who entered Oklahoma on a covered wagon and liked to write in a journal of her daily experiences. It tells of a teenager committed to becoming a teacher and **scholar**, and fighting for truth and justice. It tells of a young woman maturing into a great writer and scholar, the most prominent in her field in the entire world.

With drive, commitment, work, and intellect, each of us can make our own chosen prairie a great home.

Introduction

Oklahoman Angie Debo (1890-1988) is perhaps the best known **historian** from Oklahoma. Her **scholarship** has examined American Indian history, particularly American Indian history in Oklahoma. More Oklahomans, especially young people, need to learn Angie Debo's story. We see reminders of Debo throughout the state. Her portrait hangs in the Oklahoma State Capitol, Edmond has the Angie Debo Elementary School, and the Stillwater Public Library has a statue of her in front of the library.

At the age of eight and again at eleven, Debo kept a daily diary for three months at a time. This was her mother's idea. Children today, especially third and fourth graders, keep diaries and journals in school. Angie Debo kept her diary over 100 years ago. By reading this book, students will gain a deeper appreciation for Debo and her work as they write about their own lives.

What is the connection between Angie Debo, the daughter of **sharecroppers** from Kansas, and Oklahoma's Native American history? As a child, Debo noted that she did not encounter many American Indian people in her community. Yet, American Indian people were all around her in Oklahoma. In fact, Oklahoma means "red people" in Choctaw. As historians David Baird and Danney Goble have written in *Oklahoma, A History*, "One of the things that makes Oklahoma so unusual as a state is the long and continuous presence of Native American peoples".

American Indian communities have been present on this land long before there was an Oklahoma. Ancestors of today's Wichita and Affiliated Tribes are considered the first inhabitants of this land. By the sixteenth century, the Wichitas lived in villages along the Arkansas, Canadian, Washita, and Red rivers. The Wichitas had a **matrilineal** society, meaning that they traced their family relationships through women. And then the Plains Apaches, the Comanches, and the Osages joined them.

The story of American Indian people in Oklahoma has a distinct place in American history. Oklahoma has the largest Indian population in the United States, second only to California. Oklahoma became a state in 1907 and brought together Indian Territory

Angie Debo's mother Lina encouraged Angie to keep a diary for three months at a time and then copy it in her best handwriting. Angie considered herself a "lazy" child and did not like this task. Interestingly, she went on to keep a daily diary as an adult, always recording the weather and her daily activities. Angie's mother encouraged her daughter's writing ability at an early age. She kept all of her notebooks and report cards. In fact, her mother signed all of Angie's report cards.
B63 F63.3, ca. 1904, Angie Debo Collection, Archives, OSU Library, Oklahoma State University, Stillwater.

and Oklahoma Territory. Indian Territory had been a place where the federal government removed Indian nations; first, the **Five Tribes** in the late 1820s and 1830s and then the Plains tribes after the Civil War.

Oklahoma is also the place of the land runs. The government opened the Unassigned Lands in 1889 and the Cherokee Outlet in 1893. The Unassigned Lands had been taken from the Creeks and the Seminoles following the Civil War. Angie Debo and her family would purchase land in the Unassigned Lands and settle in Oklahoma in 1899. She would grow up to become an American Indian historian and activist for civil rights, especially American Indian issues.

This map shows the migration of the Debo family from Beattie and Welcome, Kansas, to Marshall, Oklahoma Territory, in the 1890s. As Debo writes in *A History of the Indians of the United States*, "in many ways the history of Oklahoma Indians is an epitome of Indian history." Native American communities have lived on this land long before there was a state of Oklahoma.

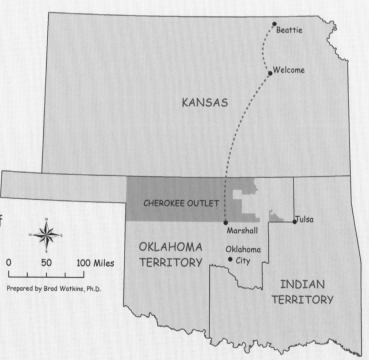

Chapter I   Daughter of the Prairie

Angie Debo's love of people began at an early age. She was born on a small leased farm near Beattie in Geary County, Kansas. In the 1890s, children in rural areas were born at home, not in hospitals. On January 30, 1890, her father, Edward, and her mother, Lina, celebrated the birth of their daughter. Angie called them Papa and Mama. She was the first born, almost two years before her brother Edwin.

The Debo family lived in Beattie until Angie was five and a half years old. The family moved three times while in Kansas in an attempt to gain enough money to purchase a farm of their own. The reason they had to move so often was that they were sharecroppers. A sharecropper would have to give one-third of the annual

Angie, right, and her brother Edwin Debo in 1893. This studio portrait was taken when the family was living in Kansas. Angie was about three years old in this photo and Edwin was almost a year old. *B63 F62.2, Angie Debo Collection, Archives, OSU Library, Oklahoma State University, Stillwater.*

crop to the landowner. This was the way that young farmers had to start out in order to build enough **capital** to buy land of their own.

The Debo family lived in this home in Welcome, Kansas, in the 1890s.
B63 F68.8, Angie Debo Collection, Archives, OSU Library, Oklahoma State University, Stillwater.

Kansas farmers were facing hard times as the depression of 1893 lowered prices for wheat and corn. Despite the depression, the Debo family managed to purchase railroad land in Welcome, Kansas. Welcome was twenty miles south of Manhattan. The Debo family sold this land four years later for a profit. They moved to Oklahoma Territory.

Mama helped a great deal in the field, as farm women did. Angie's parents used to take the buggy out to the field. This gave Angie and Edwin a shady spot to play while they worked. After the family came to Oklahoma, Mama did not work in the field. Instead, she raised a garden. Angie helped her. Mama also raised chickens and turkeys.

Mama loved to piece quilts. She pieced so many quilts when she was a girl that she still had quilt pieces that were not made up into quilts. Whenever she needed a quilt during her married life, she had those blocks already pieced. Mama gave Angie a **thimble** on her fifth birthday. With the thimble, Angie began helping Mama with the quilting.

Papa loved to read. He carried his books along with him as a young man in his late teens. He left home and started working in Nebraska and Kansas. He **husked** corn. All of his possessions were in a trunk and he had some books in the trunk. He never read a book but once. He would say, "What was the use of reading it again?"

Many daily activities depended on the weather. Sometimes the wind would blow so hard in Kansas that Mama could not dry the clothes. And the wind blew so hard Angie and Edwin could hardly walk to school.

Every Sunday the Debo family would go to church, to "preaching," as Angie called it, and Sunday school. Angie would record the title of the lesson in her diary. On Sunday evenings, Angie and Edwin would attend young folks meeting at church. Sometimes Sunday school or young folks meeting would not meet due to rain.

A Debo family portrait taken in 1898. From left: Edward, Edwin, Angie, and Lina Debo. *B63 F62.3, Angie Debo Collection, Archives, OSU Library, Oklahoma State University, Stillwater.*

From time to time Angie and Edwin had to miss Sunday school. One time the yellow Heifer had a calf. They did not go to Sunday school or to preaching because they had to take care of the calf. They hated to miss Sunday school.

Angie and Edwin spent many hours of the day together running over the prairies, gathering wildflowers, and observing nature. Angie always noticed the flowers and plants. Her grandfather was so proud of her because she was so knowledgeable about plants. By age seven, Angie dreamed of the book she would write when she grew up. It would be a book about wildflowers. Angie

Mar. 22, 1898

We had a rain last night and with some hail and this morning it snowed. and this morning it was so cold mama had to warm our shoes for us to put on and the children played in the schoolroom and made so much noise that the teacher had to tell them so many times not to make so much noise and while we was going up to school the wind blew through our stockings We practiced our pieces for the last day and when school was out it was ten minutes after four and we waited for papa and came home backwards papa tried to shoot a goose but the gun wouldnt go off

Angie Debo

Angie worked with Papa in the fields and helped Mama with domestic chores. Mama would clean the house. Sometimes, Mama would churn butter. Angie was in charge of washing and drying the dishes. *Angie Debo Collection, Archives, OSU Library, Oklahoma State University, Stillwater.*

April 7, 1898

Mama got the toothache this afternoon We butchered and didnt have dinner till about two oclock Papa went to the field and it sprinkled a little and he thought it was going to rain and he came back and took the hog down and went to the field again yesterday mama found a turkey hens nest Weather cool and windy

Angie Debo

One evening Papa heard a noise and saw something run up the tree near the house. He got the gun and shot it. It was a skunk. On another day, Angie wrote in her diary, "Papa tried to shoot a goose but the gun wouldn't go off." *Angie Debo Collection, Archives, OSU Library, Oklahoma State University, Stillwater.*

wanted to describe the plants that grew on the Kansas prairies. "I never wrote a word out of it," Angie said, "but I did practice on the title page in my newly found penmanship. It was great big fancy capitals. I always thought I would like to write."

Some evenings after supper, Papa and Mama would tell stories. Angie would write them in her diary. Other times, Mama would pop popcorn. Angie and Edwin would draw pictures with their eyes closed and stay up until nine o'clock. Other evenings, Angie and Edwin took baths in the washtub.

Angie and Edwin received one book per year from Papa and Mama. On April 20, 1898, the Debo family went to Junction City, Kansas. Mama visited the dentist and had her tooth pulled. She had suffered from a toothache for a long time. She felt much better after the dentist removed her tooth. The day was also important to Angie because her parents purchased *Uncle Tom's Cabin* by Harriet Beecher Stowe for her. They bought the book *Mother Goose* for Edwin. On April 22, 1898, Angie wrote, "I don't like *Uncle Tom's*

16

Cabin very well but mama says the rest of the book is better. I've only read the first chapter." As Angie read more chapters in the book about slavery, she liked it better. On May 4, 1898, Angie's diary entry stated: "I like *Uncle Tom's Cabin* very much. The chapters I like the best are The Husband and Father, Showing the Feelings of Living Property on Changing Owners, Escape of Eliza." At the end of a diary entry, she always signed her name, "Angie Debo." Reading about the injustices of slavery at such a young age may have helped shape Angie's later work as a historian and activist for social justice.

April 11, 1898

"Old Daisy wouldn't let her calf suck. Mama and Edwin went down there and mama tried to hold her and she couldn't and mama was afraid she would strike her with her horns. She kept horning at her calf so. Our old sow had eleven pigs and it was so cool they all chilled to death but five and it looked so much like rain papa brought them all in."

Angie Debo

Chapter 2   Going to School

Like other children in Kansas, Angie began attending school in a rural one-room schoolhouse. She began learning to read and found it to be a great joy to learn new words. "I loved to read. And I loved books," she said.

Angie enjoyed attending school. She had a wonderful teacher. Her teacher instructed fifty students of all ages. Some students were five or six years old. They were the beginners. Other students were sixteen or seventeen years old. The older students helped the little ones.

Angie enjoyed school so much that first year. She knew then that when she grew up and turned sixteen she was going to become a teacher. Sixteen was the legal age for a teacher in Kansas.

Students would take turns assisting the teacher with various chores at the schoolhouse. Sometimes students stacked wood for the stove. Often the teacher would begin the day's lesson by writing a song or **quotation** on the board. Students would copy it.

At recess, Angie and the other children would play games such as tag or rotten egg.

Angie remembered when her friend Celia Maguire moved away. Celia's father bought a farm about nine miles away. Celia had to attend a new school because her new home was so far away. On Celia's last day of school, students took turns shaking her hand. They told her they would miss her.

March 21, 1898, was a busy day at school because the students or "scholars" were taking exams. As Angie wrote in her diary, "We had **examination** in our school today. The girls dug caves at recess because they had nothing else to play. The teacher forgot to call roll."

Once examinations were over, it was all about preparing for the end-of-the-year school activities. The teacher and the older scholars made flowers out of paper to decorate the schoolroom for the last day of school. On March 23, 1898, Angie noted, "We practiced our pieces, songs and quotations and it was nine o'clock before we were done speaking. The teacher said that we would stop our program. While the teacher was calling the roll, Ida Benson would not say her quotation. The teacher told her what her quotation was and she would not say it. The teacher made her stand on the floor till all the rest had said their quotations. She wouldn't say hers and

This studio portrait features Angie and Edwin, about 1900. Angie was ten years old and Edwin was almost nine. Although they appear very formal in this image, we know that they enjoyed the outdoors, often climbing trees and fishing for perch in the creek. *B63 F62.1, Angie Debo Collection, Archives, OSU Library, Oklahoma State University, Stillwater.*

the teacher said she must say it after school was out. And then she said it."

The last day of school was such a special day, a "holiday," as Angie described it. The scholars had been practicing their pieces, quotations, and songs for several days. In the afternoon, students recited their pieces, songs and quotations. Before they sang the last song, the teacher gave each student a gift. Edwin's was tied together with yellow cord. Angie's was tied with pink cord. Students received candy and oranges from the teacher. The students presented the teacher with a special album. Angie and Edwin helped pay for the album. At the end of the day, the teacher presented the examination cards, or report cards, to the students.

In November 1899, Angie and her family moved to Marshall, Oklahoma Territory. They arrived ten years after the first and most famous land run of April 22, 1889. Her parents bought a farm near Marshall. This image features the bustling main street of Marshall in 1902. *B64 F101.2, Angie Debo Collection, Archives, OSU Library, Oklahoma State University, Stillwater.*

Chapter 3   Coming to Oklahoma

Angie and her family came to Oklahoma Territory ten years after the first and most famous land run of April 22, 1889. During the land run, people had crossed Indian lands on all sides waiting to enter and stake a **claim**. Did you know that between the "Oklahoma Lands" and Kansas was a sixty-mile outlet, or strip, still belonging to the Cherokee people? It was called the Cherokee Outlet and leased by the Cherokees to cowmen. The U.S. government had promised Cherokees the land in the Treaty of New Echota in 1835. The promise was made before their removal from their homelands to Indian Territory along the Trail of Tears. Then the U.S. government pressured the tribes to divide their land, especially following the Civil War in the mid-1860s. The opening of the Cherokee Outlet took place in 1893. It was an exciting time for settlers participating in the land runs of 1889 and the early 1890s. However, it was devastating to the tribes losing their lands.

Early settlers had lived in **dugouts**. Next came sod houses and houses made of wood. Families planted gardens and some even planted orchards. Most **homesteaders** had a cow and some chickens. By the time settlers arrived in Oklahoma Territory, schools, churches, businesses, and homes were already established in some areas.

Papa and Mama had known several families who had moved to Oklahoma Territory. They encouraged Papa to consider the move too. So the Debo family traveled through the Cherokee Outlet to get to their new home in Marshall, Oklahoma Territory, in 1899.

Papa came first in a **buckboard** with the farm equipment piled in the back. Mama, Angie, and Edwin followed in a small wagon. They sat together on the front seat. The wagon was piled high with furniture, dishes, utensils, canned fruit, clothing, and a few books. Angie and Edwin would often climb out of the wagon and walk to break up the long ride. Angie was nine and Edwin was seven at the time.

Angie often recalled that special day, "We arrived on November 8, 1899, and I have a distinct memory of the warm, sunny day, the lively little new town, and the greening wheat fields we passed as we lumbered slowly down the road to our new home."

When the Debo family moved to Oklahoma, they did not come alone. Grandmother Angeline came with them. Angie's favorite aunt, Bertrella Rosina, better known as Bird, came too. Angie's relatives made their homes nearby.

Angie's family was like so many families looking for a way out of **tenancy**. Angie's parents wanted to own their own land. At the same time, they also wanted to bring some items with them to their new home in Oklahoma Territory to remind them of Kansas. Often families would bring some of their flower cuttings with them and replant them in the gardens of their new homes. Mama and Papa brought old fashioned roses and other plants from the old home. "Here's a little Kansas soil," Mama would say. Families would divide up the cuttings and share them with each other. Each time the Debo family moved to a new home, Papa would bring a piece of lilac from the old home and plant it.

When Angie came to Oklahoma with her family, she hoped to see some Indians. She was very disappointed because she didn't. Instead, she saw homesteaders and a few cowboys who had become homesteaders. Chances are Angie did encounter Native American adults and children during her move and while growing up in Marshall. Perhaps Angie did not recognize Native communities all around her in Oklahoma Territory and Indian Territory and identify them as such. Later as an adult and historian of Native American history, she would research and write books. Many books were about the complicated relationship between the tribes and the federal government.

There was a lot of work to do. Papa made some improvements to the farm right away. He brought some elm trees up from the creek and planted them for shade. Mama, Angie, and Edwin helped too. The family fixed the house and dug a well for water. They built a barn and made a hog lot. They fenced the pasture.

Big bronze Turkey

White Leghorn

White Holland turkeys

Silver Seabright bantam

The Debo family had many animals. Papa bought Angie and Edwin a pony. They named her Queen. They also had four horses, named Nellie, Fred, Frank, and Bill. The family brought Fred and Bill with them on the move from Kansas.

They had four cows and four calves. They also had four little pigs and twenty young chickens. They had two birds and a cat named Blue Bell.

In the spring, Papa went to the town of Crescent, south of their home, and bought many fruit trees. He planted a big orchard. Angie loved to see him plant a tree. He tucked it in when he planted it. He tucked it in so affectionately.

As a child, Angie dreamed of becoming an **author**. Her mother supported Angie's goal of one day becoming an author. To encourage Angie, her mother asked her to write in her diary. In March 1901, Angie began writing daily entries in her diary again. This was a project that she had started at her mother's encouragement when she was eight. Her mother had challenged her to keep a daily diary for three months. At the time, she did not enjoy the project much. But three years later, she enjoyed reading her earlier entries. Now she was eleven and living in Oklahoma. She would start the writing project again.

Angie remembered so well when the flowers started to bloom. She found the first flower near their farm March 2, 1901, and wrote about it in her diary. Flowers bloomed much earlier in Oklahoma than in northern Kansas where she had lived.

Angie and Edwin walked everywhere as children. They relied on each other for company and **companionship**. In Oklahoma they had a creek on their farm. Angie and Edwin enjoyed walking along the creek, climbing trees, and observing the birds. Angie didn't care about dolls when she was a little girl. She would rather be

outside. When Mama would call them to come in for dinner, Angie and Edwin would be up in a tree somewhere.

Mama enjoyed the prairie landscape and the wonders of nature too. On one particularly beautiful day, the family traveled through wheat country on their horse-drawn cart. The wheat was ripe and the corn was tall and green. The sky was so blue and Mama said, "When I look out on the country like this, the tears come to my eyes. I don't know why." And the children felt it just as deeply. Angie didn't know if her father felt the same way or not.

47

May 30, 1901
We didn't go any-where but staid to home and planted sweet potatoes it was so cold mama made us wear our shoes but of course it was awful silly Papa finished the potatoes and corn
Weather — Cold .
Angie Debo

May 31, 1901
Papa mama Edwin and I all took went to Marshall and took in the oldest chickens there was only eleven left they weighed 1½ lbs apiece and 12¢ a pound when we were coming back we ahled mr, Rice and we picked a lot of mulberries
Weather — Cold
Angie Debo

June 1, 1901
Grandpa came here today Papa listed It seems rather odd to think of listing after the corn is all cultivated but he listed up the oats
Weather — Warm
Angie Debo

As farmers, the Debo family was always working. Papa raised corn and wheat. He raised a lot of corn to feed their cattle and horses. Mama would plant cabbage and tomatoes in boxes. Angie and Edwin would help their parents, and still find time to play near the creek. Angie and Edwin enjoyed playing games such as fox and geese, hide and seek, and wood tag. *Angie Debo Collection, Archives, OSU Library, Oklahoma State University, Stillwater.*

Papa worked hard. He didn't talk about it much. Angie remembered one time when Papa was driving his horses to the **binder** when he was cutting wheat. The birds nested in the wheat field just the same as they had nested in the tall grass of the prairie. When a bird would fly up, Papa would stop the binder and carry the nest to a place that he already had cut. Angie did not know if the nests had eggs or young birds in them. He saved birds that way. So maybe he did feel the same way about the landscape as the rest of the family did.

Angie's diary entry on March 4, 1901, shows a typical day of family chores and some time for fun. "We helped Papa load up some oats today. He wanted to plant them. I was going to make a playhouse but it was too cold. Mama was going to plant a garden but it was too windy so we got out of that job. Edwin blew on his mouth-organ to-night and told me to write it and I will to please him."

Wheat tends to handle drought better than other crops. When Papa raised wheat, the **threshing machine** would come in the summer. The wheat was cut and **shocked**, or placed in bundles. Papa cut it and shocked it himself. Sometimes he would hire someone to help him shock it. It would be in shocks (bundles) so that it would stand out against the rain until the threshing machine came. The threshing removed the grains and seeds from the cut wheat. Most of the wheat would be stored in the **granary** until winter. Papa would haul the wheat to Hennessey.

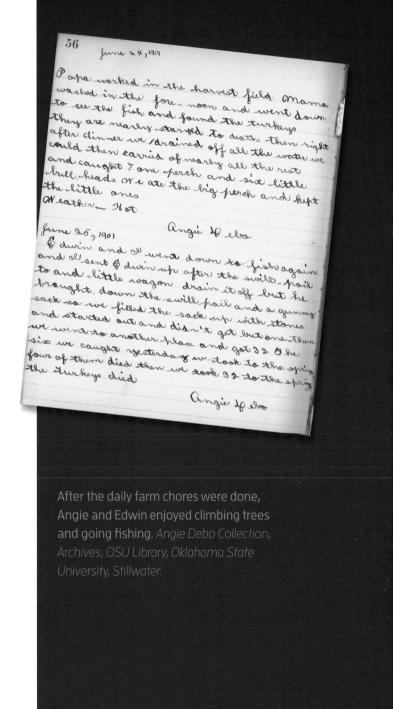

After the daily farm chores were done, Angie and Edwin enjoyed climbing trees and going fishing. *Angie Debo Collection, Archives, OSU Library, Oklahoma State University, Stillwater.*

Hauling a load of wheat or oats to Hennessey was an all-day event. They took the horses and hitched them to the wagon. Hennessey was 15 miles away, or thirty miles round trip. As Angie recorded in her diary on March 12, 1901, "We went to Hennessey with a load of oats. It was the second time I've ever been there. Mama got two teeth drawn. I got a hat too. We were too early. There was only one store with trimmed hats in it. Edwin got a pair of shoes. When we went over to town we had to face an awful hard wind. Weather — warm and terrible windy."

In May and June of 1901, Angie and Edwin went fishing a few times in the nearby ponds and lakes. First, they caught four fish in their neighbor's pond. "I caught the biggest one with my hands," Angie wrote in her diary, "and was going to take it home but we put it where it couldn't get away and it got away any-how." Two days later, Papa went fishing with Angie and Edwin. Angie wrote, "we fished and fished and fished all the fore-noon and didn't catch anything."

A month later they tried fishing again and caught one perch and six little bull heads. "We ate the big perch," Angie wrote in her diary, "and kept the little ones." Angie and Edwin were fond of catching fish like perch in the creek and preparing them for dinner.

Angie and Edwin loved to climb trees. They found a tree near a creek and played in its branches. They were looking for a place where Papa could build a playhouse. When Angie and Edwin found the perfect spot on the farm to build their playhouse, Angie remembered feeling like a true Oklahoman.

The Debo family worked hard to farm their land and make their house a home. They built a barn, planted trees, fenced the pasture, dug a well, and made a hog lot. Like their neighbors, they had some cows, horses and mules, hogs, and chickens. They had a vegetable garden. They planted onions, potatoes, tomatoes, and other vegetables. From time to time, Angie's father provided meat for the family meal by hunting rabbits, wild turkeys, and deer.

Chapter 4   Making Oklahoma Home

Angie and Edwin attended school at Rosenberg School, six miles southwest of Marshall, in Logan County, Oklahoma Territory. The new frame schoolhouse replaced the original sod schoolhouse from the land run days. When Angie and Edwin arrived in Marshall, school was held from April to June. As the community developed and grew, the school year increased to six months.

How did children get to school? Many of them walked to school or rode their ponies. Angie and Edwin rode their pony Queen to school. Other children were picked up for school by the kid wagon. The kid wagon was a long platform with seats on the sides covered by a roof. It was drawn

Angie and Edwin with their teacher and classmates at Rosenberg School District No. 97, the one-room schoolhouse southwest of Marshall, Oklahoma Territory, about 1902. On the right, Angie and her brother Edwin stand on either side of their pony Queen. Angie and Edwin rode Queen to school. Other "scholars," as the students were called, were picked up for school by the kid wagon, a covered cart pulled by horses. *B63 F60.1, Angie Debo Collection, Archives, OSU Library, Oklahoma State University, Stillwater.*

by horses or mules. Everyone in the community called it the kid wagon.

Teachers were young women, often teenagers, who had passed their examinations to teach. The teachers would **board** in the home of a family who lived near the school.

Angie enjoyed going to school. In Kansas, she was so eager to learn that she sat in the front row of Miss Gleason's classroom. Miss Gleason recognized Angie's desire for reading and encouraged her to stay

For her part, Angie received special permission from her teacher to bring a notebook to school to record all of her lessons and assignments. At the time, chalk on slate boards was the standard. Here is a map Angie made showing Marshall and other towns in Logan County, Oklahoma Territory. *Angie Debo Collection, Archives, OSU Library, Oklahoma State University, Stillwater.*

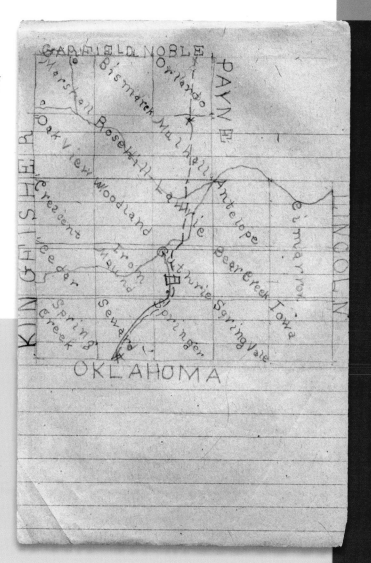

after school for additional reading instruction. Angie's first teacher in Marshall was Mrs. Noble, a widow with two little girls. She lived on a farm near the school.

Like Angie and Edwin, many of the children enjoyed school and loved books. Books were scarce and considered treasures to handle with care. Students and their families had to purchase their books for school. Angie kept all of the books that she used in school including her McGuffey Reader textbooks. "I had all the books I needed," Angie remembered. "My parents bought them."

The schoolhouse was the community center for meetings, music lessons, student performances, Sunday school, pie socials, and box suppers.

On Sundays, the school house served as the meeting place for Sunday school. In her diary, Angie would include the weekly entry on Sunday school. She listed the title of the lesson and the young folks meeting in the evening. Sunday evenings were also dedicated to visiting, hosting neighbors and relatives in the Debo home, or visiting family and friends nearby. During these visits, families would play games, sing songs, have a meal together, and share stories.

An example of a family story that the Debo family would share was the "**kerosene**" story. They would tell the kerosene story when family and friends would visit. They would always laugh about it.

Angie's mother had sent the children to town, to Marshall, to buy a sack of flour and a can of kerosene.

They used the kerosene for their lamps and their mother instructed them how to transport it back home in the horse-drawn cart. Somehow Angie and Edwin forgot. They put the flour sack down in the bottom of the cart and placed the kerosene on top of it. On the way home, some kerosene spilled. When they got home there was a spot on the flour sack where the kerosene can had been.

Angie's mother couldn't throw the whole sack of flour away. She **discarded** a portion of it and kept the rest. As long as that sack of flour lasted, her mother's good bread tasted of kerosene. But, the family had to eat it! They did not have money to buy any more flour.

By the time Debo was a teenager, she realized that the story—and the telling of the story—was her first experience in understanding the Oklahoma spirit. She said to her parents, "Did you notice that none of us had to explain why we had to eat damaged food because there wasn't any money to buy more? We all understood each other and we laughed about it—well, that was a universal experience that Oklahomans had."

The kerosene story illustrated what Angie considered to be a universal, or shared, experience. It was the story of homesteaders and the community they founded. It is also a story of shared experience and the making of an American community.

Conclusion Historical Significance of Angie Debo

If you ever visit Oklahoma and explore the State Capitol, you will see Angie Debo's portrait hanging next to famous Oklahomans such as Will Rogers, Sequoyah, Jim Thorpe, and Carl Albert. Angie Debo had the honor of having her portrait in the Oklahoma State Capitol. She was a historian. She wrote about Oklahoma and its people, but especially American Indian people.

Born in Kansas in 1890, as a young girl she moved to Marshall in Oklahoma Territory with her family as part of a larger migration – people in search of a better life and land ownership. Her educational experience began in rural one-room schools in Kansas and Oklahoma.

She attended the University of Oklahoma and received the majority of her training from E. E. Dale, a student of western historian Frederick Jackson Turner, and her work reflects this tradition. She then attended graduate school in international relations at the University of Chicago. Her master's thesis, *The Historical Background of the American Policy of Isolation*, was published in 1924. She attained the doctorate in history with Dale at the University of Oklahoma while working at the demonstration school and the museum at West Texas State Teachers' College. Although her dissertation, *The Rise and Fall of the Choctaw Republic*, received the John H. Dunning Prize of the American Historical

Angie Debo, seated front row, received the common school diploma at the age of twelve and the teacher's certificate at the age of sixteen. She taught in rural schools as a teenager while she waited for Marshall to build a high school. *Angie Debo Collection, Archives, OSU Library, Oklahoma State University, Stillwater.*

Association in 1934 as the most important contribution to studies in American history, Debo never held a tenure-track position as a history professor.

During the Depression years, Debo continued applying for academic posts without success and turned her attention toward a career as a professional writer. She supported herself through part-time employment and grants, and by living within limited means with her parents in rural

Oklahoma. In a back room of the family home, Debo would write stories of Oklahoma's Indians and pioneers on her typewriter. Her personal **motto** was "discover the truth and publish it." This provided Debo with the ability to tell the stories of Oklahoma's people.

"I didn't do anything except write," Debo reflected in 1983, "except once in a while if I needed money and had to work for a time to earn a little." Debo

One of the drawbacks of moving to Marshall in Oklahoma Territory was the lack of a high school for Angie (pictured on the far left). Once the high school was established, Angie participated in the first graduating class, the Class of 1913, graduating from Marshall High School at the "advanced age" of twenty-three. But this did not stop her determination for education and her love of books. *B64 F102.01, Angie Debo Collection, Archives, OSU Library, Oklahoma State University, Stillwater.*

continued publishing important studies, including the controversial and, to Debo, "most important" work, *And Still the Waters Run*. It told the story of the **dissolution** of Five Tribes' lands and government.

During her professional writing career, Debo wrote nine books, coauthored one, and edited three. In addition, she published over one hundred articles and book reviews on American Indian history and Oklahoma history. Debo studied American Indian history by using a variety of sources, including oral tradition, to present what she believed to be more accurate scholarship.

Angie Debo lived to be 98 years old. She left a legacy at the local level in her hometown of Marshall, at the state level within the halls of the capitol building, and at the national level as a historian. The documentary film, *"Indians, Outlaws and Angie Debo"* describes the work of Angie Debo as an author and activist.

After her death, Angie Debo's papers and the **transcripts** of the oral history interviews were deposited in Archives at the library at Oklahoma State University. Through this manuscript collection, today's scholars can trace the path Angie Debo followed as a historian.

Angie Debo's life and writings continue to inspire us. She brings us together in community as we renew our commitment to following her trail.

Glossary

author—a person who writes

binder—an attachment to a harvester/reaper to bind the cut grain

board—to furnish with meals/lodging

buckboard—four-wheeled carriage

capital—wealth; money/property

claim—something that is claimed, such as a piece of land

companionship—friendly relationship

culture—the quality in a person or society

discarded—to cast aside or dispose of

dissolution—the undoing or breaking of a bond/partnership

dugout—a shelter/dwelling formed in the ground

examination—a test

Five Tribes—Choctaws, Chickasaws, Cherokees, Creeks, Seminoles

granary—a storehouse for grain

historian—an expert in history

homesteaders—a settler; the owner of a homestead

husked—to remove the husk from harvested corn

kerosene—a liquid mixture used as fuel

matrilineal—tracing family relationships through the women

motto—a person's guiding principle

quotation—a passage quoted from a book, speech, etc.

scholar—a student

scholarship—learning; knowledge acquired by study

sharecropper—a tenant farmer who pays as rent a share of the crop

shocked—bundles/stacks of grain stalks in the field waiting threshing

tenancy—a piece of land used by a sharecropper

thimble—a small cap worn on the fingertip to protect when pushing a needle through cloth in sewing

threshing machine—a machine for removing grains and seeds from straw and chaff

transcripts—official copies or records

Places to Visit

Gaylord-Pickens Museum, home of the
Oklahoma Hall of Fame
1400 Classen Drive
Oklahoma City, Oklahoma 73106
oklahomahof.com

Oklahoma State Capitol
2300 N. Lincoln Boulevard
Oklahoma City, Oklahoma 73105

Oklahoma History Center
800 Nazih Zuhdi Drive
Oklahoma City, Oklahoma 73105
okhistory.org

Archives
Edmon Low Library
Oklahoma State University
Stillwater, Oklahoma 74075
info.library.okstate.edu/scua/home

Stillwater Public Library
1107 S. Duck Street
Stillwater, Oklahoma 74074
library.stillwater.org

Timeline: Historian Angie Debo (1890-1988)

1890	Angie Debo was born January 30, 1890, in Beattie, Kansas
1899	Family moved from Kansas to Marshall, Oklahoma Territory
1902	Received the common school diploma at age 12
1907	Oklahoma statehood
1907-10	Received the teacher's certificate and taught in one-room schoolhouses near Marshall in Logan and Garfield counties
1913	Graduated with the first graduating class from Marshall High School at the age of 23
1918	Graduated with the B.A. in history from the University of Oklahoma
1924	Earned M.A. in history from the University of Chicago
1924-33	Instructed future teachers at the demonstration school, West Texas State Teachers College
1933	Earned Ph.D. in history from the University of Oklahoma
1934	Published *The Rise and Fall of the Choctaw Republic*
1935	Received the John H. Dunning Prize from the American Historical Association for *The Rise and Fall of the Choctaw Republic*
1940	Published *And Still the Waters Run*
1941	Published *The Road to Disappearance*
1947-55	Served on the faculty at Oklahoma A&M College (later Oklahoma State University) as curator of maps
1973	Received the Distinguished Service Award from the Oklahoma Hall of Fame
1981-85	Interviewed many times over four years for the oral history project at Oklahoma State University
1985	Honored by the State of Oklahoma with her portrait placed in the Rotunda of the Oklahoma State Capitol
1988	Passed away PBS documentary "Indians, Outlaws, and Angie Debo" aired

Bibliography

Angie Debo Collection, Archives, Oklahoma State University Library, Oklahoma State University Library.

    About Angie Debo, http://info.library.okstate.edu/debo/bio

    Angie Debo Collection, http://info.library.okstate.edu/debo

    The Angie Debo Collection at Oklahoma State University includes the Angie Debo Papers, images, finding aids, oral history interviews, and other helpful resources.

Dr. Angie Debo by Charles Banks Wilson, Teaching with Capitol Art, Oklahoma Arts Council

http://www.arts.ok.gov/Art_at_the_Capitol/Capitol_Collection/Wilson/Dr_Angie_Debo.html

    The Oklahoma Arts Council's Teaching with Capitol Art site includes an examination of Angie Debo's portrait and the Oklahoma State Capitol along with information about the artist Charles Banks Wilson and teacher resources.

"Angie Debo: Teacher, Historian and Author." Voices of Oklahoma, Oklahoma Center for the Humanities,

    University of Tulsa, March 24, 2017, http://www.voicesofoklahoma.com/interview/debo-angie/

Baird, W. David and Danney Goble. *Oklahoma: A History.* Norman: University of Oklahoma Press, 2008.

Debo, Angie. *And Still the Waters Run: The Betrayal of the Five Civilized Tribes.* Princeton: Princeton University Press, 1940.

Debo, Angie. *A History of Indians of the United States.* Norman: University of Oklahoma Press, 1970.

Leckie, Shirley A. *Angie Debo: Pioneering Historian.* Norman: University of Oklahoma Press, 2000.

Loughlin, Patricia. *Hidden Treasures of the American West: Muriel H. Wright, Angie Debo, and Alice Marriott.* Albuquerque: University of New Mexico Press, 2005.

Reese, Linda Williams. *Women of Oklahoma, 1890-1920.* Norman: University of Oklahoma Press, 1997.

Index

_____, Angeline (grandmother) 22

_____, Bertrella Rosina (aunt) 22

Albert, Carl 34

American Historical Association 34-35; John H. Dunning Prize 34

And Still the Waters Run 36

Angie Debo Elementary School 8

Arkansas River 9

Baird, David 8

Beattie, KS 10-11

Canadian River 9

Cherokee Outlet 10, 21-22

Cherokee Tribe 21

Choctaw Tribe 8

Civil War 10, 21

Comanche Tribe 9

Creek Tribe 10

Dale, E.E. 34

Debo, Angie 6-37

Debo, Edward (father) 11, 13-16, 22-24, 26-29, 33

Debo, Edwin (brother) 11, 13-14, 16-17, 19-20, 22-30, 32-33

Debo, Lina (mother) 9, 11, 13-17, 22-26, 28-29, 23-33

Five Tribes 10

Goble, Danney 8

Hennessey, O.T. 27-28

Henry, Robert 6-7

Historical Background of the American Policy of Isolation, The 34

History of the Indians in the United States, A 10

Indian Territory 9-10

Indians Outlaws and Angie Debo 37

Junction City, KS 16

Maguire, Celia 18

Manhattan, KS 10

Marshall, O.T./OK 6, 10, 20, 22-23, 30-32, 34-37; High School 36

McGuffey Reader textbooks 32

Mother Goose 16

Oklahoma State Capitol 6-8, 34; Rotunda 6

Oklahoma State University 6 9, 11-12, 14-15, 19-20, 26-27, 30-31, 35-37

Oklahoma Territory 10, 12, 21-23, 34, 36

Oklahoma, A History 8

Osage Tribe 9

Plains Apache Tribe 9

Red River 9

Rise and Fall of the Choctaw Republic, The 34

Rogers, Will 34

Rosenberg School District No. 97, O.T. 30

Seminole Tribe 10

Sequoyah 34

Stillwater Public Library 8

Stowe, Harriet Beecher 16

Thorpe, Jim 34

Trail of Tears 21

Treaty of New Echota 21

Turner, Frederick Jackson 34

Unassigned Lands 10

Uncle Tom's Cabin 16-17

University of Chicago 34

University of Oklahoma 34

Washita River 9

Welcome, KS 10, 12

West Texas State Teachers' College 34

Wichita Tribe 9

Williams, Penny 6-7

Wilson, Charles Banks 6